MONEY MADE $IMPLE ©

Easy Answers
To Tough Money Questions

Angie Hollerich CEP, CCA

Foreward written by
Joseph T. Deters, Ohio Treasurer of State

ISBN # 0-9679681-4-3
Money Made $imple, Easy Answers to Tough Money Questions.
2004 Edition

Retail price: $12.95

Published by Brass Ring Productions
P. O. Box 307318
Gahanna, Ohio 43230-7318

Cover Design, Layout and Illustrations
Green Venus Design
dhollerich7362@wowway.com

Brass Ring Productions books are available at special discounts
for bulk purchases. For more information about how to arrange
such purchases, please contact Brass Ring Productions,
P. O. Box 307318, Gahanna, Ohio 43230-7318, or call
614-337-2204 or fax 614-337-2283, or find us by visiting
our web site www.brassringpro.com

Disclaimer: The opinions expressed herein are solely those of the
author and are based on the authors' personal experiences. They
are not intended to be the norm for all persons. Reasonable care
has been taken in the preparation of the text to ensure its clarity
and accuracy. The book is sold with the understanding that the
author and the publisher are not engaged in rendering legal or
accounting services. Laws vary from state to state, and readers
with specific financial questions should seek the serviced of a
professional advisor. The author and publisher specifically
disclaim any liability, loss or risk personal or otherwise, which
is incurred as a consequence, directly or indirectly of the use
and application of any of the contents of this book.

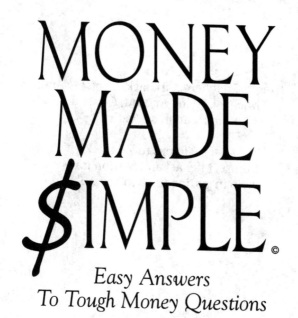

MONEY MADE $IMPLE ©

Easy Answers
To Tough Money Questions

Angie Hollerich CEP, CCA

Foreward written by
Joseph T. Deters, Ohio Treasurer of State

Love to Jack,
Greg & Gretchen, Kari, Jack, Denise & Audrey,
Michael, Heidi, Andrew, Christopher,
Hannah & Heather.

Thanks to Kari,
Denise, Michael and Marion for your
help in getting the book completed.

F O R E W O R D

To paraphrase a television commercial from yesteryear, "Angie knows money."

Angie Hollerich, the author of this fine book, truly does understand the subject of money – and especially as it relates to matters of personal finance. As she notes in her introduction, her present-day expertise on money matters arose from desperate circumstances. Too often in life, a sudden or unexpected change can leave us facing situations we're not quite prepared to handle. This happened to Angie. Her chief challenge was to begin climbing out of the financial hole she fell into after her divorce.

And climb she did. Today, Angie Hollerich is a successful entrepreneur, a popular author, an expert on personal finance, and a sought-after speaker and presenter – which is how I came to know her. In the summer of 2000, our office launched Women & Money, a series of free, personal-finance workshops tailored for women. We started in Ohio's five largest cities – Cincinnati, Cleveland, Columbus, Dayton, and Toledo. Since those humble beginnings, more than 10,000 Ohio women have attended one of our sessions. This year, 2004, our workshops will be offered 11 times around Ohio.

Women & Money is a tremendous success story. It is literally changing women's lives for the better. And Angie Hollerich has been a major reason why this has happened. We worked hard that first year back in 2000 to find the very best team of presenters we could find to conduct breakout sessions on subjects ranging from budgeting and managing credit, to home ownership. Angie was one of those "ground-floor" presenters that year. In 2001, we placed her in charge of our presenting team – a distinction she holds yet today.

Angie probably asked me to write the Forward for Money Made Simple because I've watched her in action for the last four years, answering our attendees' questions during the closing session of our workshops. No matter how personal or arcane the questions may be, she always has the right answer, or the right advice. She has told me that these closing sessions reminded her of the hundreds of times she has stood before other audiences – of women and men – and performed the same service. And, toward the end of our 2003 season, the idea dawned on her to assemble the notes she accumulated over the last 14 years and write this book.

No one individual can possibly know everything there is to know about any given subject, and I'm sure Angie would not pretend to have the answer to every conceivable question concerning money. But this book covers a very broad array of topics, and I can assure you that the information and advice provided within these covers showcase Angie Hollerich at her best.

As you turn the pages of this book, I am confident you will agree with my opening thought – Angie really does know money. And when you're finished reading, I think you will, too.

Respectfully,

Joseph T. Deters
Ohio Treasurer of State

INTRODUCTION

So many questions, so little time.

For over 15 years I have managed, consulted, advised, presented and trained thousands of men and women on how to achieve financial success. That was an interesting position to be in, since I was not financially savvy prior to my divorce in 1988. At the time, I lost 80% of my income and had to get some serious money questions answered. If only there had been a book available that addressed all of the financial questions I had! Not only the basic questions, but questions that covered all of the financial areas that I needed information on in order to achieve my financial goals.

You may have heard the saying, "It's not just knowing the answers, it's knowing the right questions to ask that matters." I have found over the years that there is really nothing new to know about managing your money, but what can be new is how the information is presented. I thought that if I wrote a book of questions and answers, it would give information to those individuals who may not know the right questions to ask.

This book answers the top questions that I have been asked over the years at seminars, conferences and trainings, and covers everything from budgeting to estate planning. My goal was to provide easy answers to your money questions. I feel I have succeeded in that goal.

Good luck with achieving your financial success.

CHAPTER 1

Budgeting

Budgeting is crucial to managing your day-to-day finances. The purpose of budgeting is to:

 • **Define possible problems in spending patterns.**

 • **Identify opportunities to overcome the problems.**

 • **Help plan a realistic way to improve your spending habits.**

It should carefully balance all of the needs of your family, so be sure to include all members in the process.

1. What is a budget?

A budget is a tool to help manage and control your spending and saving. It can be used to help you be more aware of your spending habits and behaviors. It will help you manage your income in a way that will maximize your goals, keep you on track and keep up on where you spend your money.

2. Should everyone have a budget?

Yes. No matter who you are and how much you make, keeping a budget will allow you to control your income and spending.

3. What is the first step to budgeting?

The first step is to find out where your money goes. You can do that by reconstructing your spending over the past twelve months. If you have a handle on what you buy, why you buy it and when you spend your

Write it Down!
Putting it on paper makes it real and will help you better understand where your money is really being spent.

money, you will then be able to make the necessary adjustments for the future. It is critical that you do not underestimate your spending. Look at necessities such as your house payment and utility bills vs. your entertainment expenses. Writing your bills down will help you track when they are due.

"A part of everything you earn should be yours to keep. Before you pay others, put aside money for yourself."

4. What should a budget include?

A budget should always include a plan to reduce your overall debt. In order to move forward and save, you first need to handle any debt you have. (See Credit and Debt.) It should also have real income and expense figures.

"Your current and potential income both influence just how much you can invest."

5. How do I develop a budget?

A budget should always be written down; there is something to writing it down on paper that makes it real. You will want to develop your budget based on monthly spending averages. Not all bills, however, are paid monthly—some are paid quarterly, biannually or even annually. For those, make the following calculations to determine how much you will need to save each month in order to be able to make the payments when they are due:

Annually ⟶ Divide the total payment by twelve.

Biannually ⟶ Divide the total by six.

Quarterly ⟶ Divide the total by four.

5. How do I control my budget?

Some things in your budget are controllable, if you are willing to take a little time and effort on your own behalf. Expenses are flexible; you can control your flow of spending by making sacrifices today for quality of life tomorrow. On the other hand, because your job only pays you so much, your income may be harder to control.

6. Help! I have more money going out than I have coming in. What can I do?

It's important to understand how and where you spend your money. It's only from your cash flow that you will accumulate enough money to save and invest. Take the time to fill out a cash flow work sheet. It will give you a base with which to work. You can get a cash flow sheet from your financial advisor or online from several financial sites.

7. I think I am an impulsive spender. Any suggestions for help?

If you tend to shop and purchase items impulsively for no reason, perhaps you should start thinking about what you are about to purchase before you buy it. Think about the price, where you might spend the money and how hard you have worked for the money you are using to pay for it. Some other ways to avoid impulse spending include only shopping when you have a need and always using a shopping list. If you keep to a list, you will be less likely to give into unplanned spending.

8. Why is budgeting so important?

If you guess every month when determining what money you have and what bills you pay, you are playing a dangerous game. Think about it. If your figures are off by $100 a month every month, that budgeting oversight can add up to

"It's hard to say no to ourselves; before you purchase those clothes or other merchandise, ask yourself if you really need them, and if not-- put them back."

"It's not the big expenses that hurt us, it's the little ones."

$1,200 a year. If you were to take that same $1,200, invest it and assume an 8% after-tax return, in 20 years that amount could be as much as $60,000. As you can see, a $100 a month can be a really big deal. Having a budget keeps you from making big money mistakes.

9. Doesn't having a budget just mean you have to give up the things you want to buy?

No. In reality, a budget is the tool you will use to make better spending and saving decisions. A budget should not be perceived as a problem, but a solution and a start toward achieving your financial goals.

11. What is my net worth, and why should it be a part of my budget?

First, don't confuse your net worth with your income (your income is the money that you earn when you work). Your net worth includes all of the assets you have accumulated. These are the things you own that will become more valuable over time, such as your home and investments. Many people make a lot of money, but that doesn't necessarily mean they are wealthy. Why? Because they spend every dime they make. If most of the money coming into your household gets spent and goes right back out, you are not building your net worth. You will want to invest your money in things that appreciate in value and add to the assets you already have.

"Budgeting isn't about what you make, it's about how you manage what you make."

12. How do I get family members to buy into the budgeting process?

Good question, and probably the hardest one to answer. If you and your partner clash over money and spending, there are several ways to solve the problem:

First, you both have to be willing to sit down and talk without bringing up the past.

Second, both of you should discuss what you consider the most difficult part of budgeting.

Third, be sure you're on the same path when it comes to your goals and objectives.

Fourth, be willing to negotiate with each of your family members as they bring their money issues into the family budget. Remember that some give and take is necessary for success.

How your money grows.

As you can see, the budgeting questions all address very basic but important strategies. If you are successful with your budgeting skills, you will be successful with your saving skills, because you will have extra money every month. Regular saving is essential to achieving financial security. As your income increases, savings increase also.

Select and design a budget that suits your needs.

What works for one family may not work for another. Budgets come in many forms and styles, so it should be possible to find the right fit for you. There are many budget sheets available online and in books.

Forecast your income to identify your various sources of income.

This exercise needs to be realistic, particularly when considering items of uncertain amounts or nonrecurring income, like bonuses.

Summarize past expenses.

You will not be able to predict the future without first looking at past expenses. The more precise you can be, the better your budget will work out. Use your receipts and cancelled checks to make an honest estimate of how you spend your cash. Another strategy is to carry a small journal and record each and every item purchased using cash. Because there is no record of these purchases, this is the kind of spending you'll most likely forget. "Out of sight, out of mind."

Estimate future expenses.

Now that you have taken the time to check out your past expenses, you will want to look into what your future holds. Estimate your expenses over a month, a quarter or a year. Your goal should be to spend less than you make and to get in the habit of saving regularly.

At the end of the budget period you've chosen to work with, compare your actual expenses with your estimated expenses. Once you've prepared and worked with a few budgets, you will become proficient in identifying the areas where you can reduce your expenses further. Before you know it, you will be well on your way to putting your financial house in good order.

C H A P T E R 2

Credit & Debt

Getting started on the right financial foot is essential today in order to protect yourself from financial problems that will affect your future well being. There are some problems that may be beyond your control, such as accidents or getting laid off from your job, but you can avoid many financial problems by learning to control the amount of debt you accumulate. Two strategies to achieving this include:

Getting your debts under control.
Many people take on way too much consumer debt. Whatever your debt situation, take the necessary steps to get it under control.

Maintaining good credit.
Whether you have a lot of debt, a little debt, or no debt, you need to create a good credit history so that you can access credit when you need it.

1. What is credit?

Credit is your ability to borrow money from a bank or financial company. Your have a "credit" score that tells these lenders how reliable you are. Credit is a convenient way to take care of many of your day-to-day financial transactions. You can use credit to make large purchases in a fast, easy and safe way, and it eliminates the need to carry a lot of cash.

2. How do I know if I have good credit?

It is important to review your credit report at least once a year. Check to make sure that all the accounts shown in the report are really your accounts and that the balances are correct. Some of your creditors may not be current in their reporting, so your report could show that you still owe money that has already been paid. If you have been denied credit, are unemployed or are a victim of fraud, you can get a free copy of your report.

There are three major credit bureau's:

Equifax
1-800-685-1111
P. O. Box 105496
Atlanta, GA 30348
www.equifax.com

Experian
1-800-397-3742
P. O. Box 9556
Allen Texas 75013
www.experian.com

TransUnion
1-800-888-4213
P. O. Box 1000
Chester, PA 19022
www.transunion.com

3. How many credit cards do I need?

Most of the time, you will only need one credit card. If you get an offer for another card that gives you a

"If you fall into the credit card trap, you may find yourself joining the ever increasing number of individuals that are one paycheck away from being homeless."

better interest rate, apply for it, but don't cancel the one you have until you are approved. As soon as you get the new card, cancel and destroy your other card right away.

4. What should I look for when applying for credit?

Here are the questions you should ask when applying for a credit card:

- Is there an annual fee or other fees charged for its use?
- What is the finance charge for outstanding balances?
- Is there a minimum finance charge?
- What is the grace period, and if you pay the balance off will you still be charged?
- Is the card widely accepted, or will you have limited use?
- Are there additional benefits for using the card, such as air miles?

5. I have been asked to co-sign on a credit application with a relative. What should I do?

This can be very dangerous. If anything happens and they default on the loan, your credit could be ruined. Be very careful before you decide to share credit with someone.

6. I keep receiving balance transfer deals. Should I take advantage of them?

If you have excellent credit, you will receive enticing offers stating "life-of-the-balance" credit card deals, or you might even get offered zero percent for the life of the balance. These offers usually come with promises that may sound terrific, but be very careful. Find out what you will need to do to keep the great rate offers.

Clarify the deal to make sure there are no hidden requirements, such as a minimum monthly purchase.

Be suspicious of the letter. Just because it says you have been pre-approved for a line of credit of $30,000 at 3%, doesn't mean you have been. They want you to apply, and when you do not qualify for the lower rates, they will give you the higher interest rates instead.

Watch your step. Even if the offer is real, be very careful. Read the offer

"Once you have curtailed your unnecessary spending, you have the ability to plan for a secure financial future."

23

thoroughly, especially the small print.

Remember that these credit card companies are a business; they will not lend you money at a loss. Make sure the interest rate is fixed. Variable rates may look good now that interest rates are low, but they may not look as appealing if rates increase.

Be punctual, or else. Even if you do qualify for those great low rates, pay your bills on time. If you miss a payment (missing a payment may mean paying only a day late), they can accelerate you to the worst interest rate. Most credit cards now have a clause that says if you are late, you lose your great low rate.

7. Are there warning signs to help me recognize if I have credit problems?

Credit cards are too easy to get. They are a wonderful convenience but are often abused as balances grow larger and larger. Here are some warning signals to consider:

- You have maxed out or overextended your cards.
- You cannot make even your minimum payments.
- You have no idea how much you owe.
- You fill out new applications regularly.

- You have been denied credit.
- Your creditors are calling you.
- You use credit to buy everyday necessities.

If any of these signs sound familiar, taking charge of your situation is vital.

8. I am considering debt consolidation. Is that a good idea?

Beware of offers to consolidate your debt. Primarily, their ads promise to help you with your debts, but typically these offers come from financial companies that charge a very high interest rate and spread the loan payments out over many years so you do not feel as much pain. Consider if you really want to be paying these bills over a 20-year period and paying for the items bought with this credit many times over. You do not want to take on long-term debt to pay for short-term pleasures.

If you are dead set on getting help to decrease your debt, there is help available. Contact the National Foundation for Consumer Credit. It is a network of 1,450 organizations that provide consumer education, budget and debt counseling and debt repayment programs for both families and individuals. Some are locally managed, operating under the name Consumer Credit

Counseling Service (CCCS). Call 1-800-388-2227 or visit their website www.nfcc.org. They may be able to do things for you that you cannot do for yourself, such as:

- Negotiate with the credit card companies to lower or even stop the interest on your debt.
- Establish a spending plan.
- Determine your financial options.
- Re-establish your credit.
- Arrange a debt management plan.

These agencies are non-profit and can provide services at no coast or at a fee on a sliding scale, so no one is ever turned away.

9. I am considering bankruptcy. What are the pros and cons and the different types I should know about?

Bankruptcy is a legal way to get rid of debt under federal law. Although it may sound like the only way out at times, it is an extreme measure, and should only be used as a last resort. You may think that if you file for bankruptcy it will make your creditors go away, but that is not true, and filing bankruptcy will have a negative implication on your credit record. If this is the course of action you want to take, however, you will need to understand the two types of bankruptcy.

Chapter 7. A chapter 7 bankruptcy is a straight bankruptcy and can get rid of most of your debts, but it will require that you also give up some of your assets. The court assumes legal control over your non-exempt property and the bills you owe. You will not be able to sell or pay anything without the consent of the court. You will have a court appointed trustee whose primary role is to see that your creditors are paid as much of your debt as possible. In the end, the court will discharge most of your debts and you will no longer owe your creditors. You will not be able to file another chapter 7 for six years.

Chapter 13. In a chapter 13 bankruptcy, your are not discharged from your debts. It is a process established so you can repay your debts over time. While your bankruptcy is pending, you will have to live within a strict budget established by the court and submit a repayment strategy. This type of bankruptcy is the best if you owe back taxes or are behind in your mortgage payments. Some of your planned payments may be taken out of your paycheck. Chapter 13 remains on your records for seven years although, in some cases, it may stay on for ten years. You also may be required to attend a money management program to help keep you from making the same mistake again.

10. Help, I am in so much debt! What can I do to pay off my credit?

If you want to aggressively eliminate debt, here are the issues you must address:

Are you willing to begin a cash-only spending policy, putting your credit cards away?

Will you have to save for a down payment for a major purchase soon?

Do you know the realistic time frame for paying off the debt you owe?

Are you willing to cut back on your discretionary spending and commit to a monthly budget?

Do you anticipate receiving a bonus, salary increase or inheritance?

Do you have an emergency fund for unexpected expenses?

These are the questions you must answer to start on the path to being debt free.

11. How do I re-establish my credit after I get back on my feet?

When you need to re-establish your credit, you will need to get a secured credit card. These are not easy to get, and you must find a bank that is willing to take a risk with you. You set up an account by depositing $200 to $500, and the bank will issue you a credit card for the amount you have deposited. If you default or are late in making a payment, the bank will use the money in your account to cover the amount. You will be able to apply for an unsecured credit card within twelve to eighteen months after re-establishing your credit.

12. What is the difference between good debt and bad debt?

Good debt is the debt you take on when you purchase a car, college education or a home-- something it would normally take you years to save for. With the average cost of a

"Sacrifice today for quality of life tomorrow."

"You have the ability to win the wealth battle."

home being about $150,000, it would take way too long to save the money to buy it all at once, so you take on a loan or debt to purchase it. This is good debt. Your home provides shelter and a tax deduction, a car provides much needed transportation to work to make the money to pay for the car, and the education is an investment in yourself or your children. So good debt helps you provide for the needs of your family.

Bad debt, on the other hand, is the debt you accumulate with your credit cards-- usually used to purchase items that you consume everyday, like meals out, or things that will depreciate quickly, such as tennis shoes, clothes or toys. If you have a negative net worth, it is usually because you're financing your lifestyle with credit cards and not with your paycheck. Realistically, until you reach retirement, you will still be building your liability category. Just work on building good debt and not bad debt.

As you can see, it's important to take a good look at your debt and assess how you're doing to date. Unfortunately, debt follows you around wherever you go. The decisions you make have an effect on whether or not you will be able to purchase a home, purchase a car, rent an apartment or get that job you are applying for, since potential employers or landlords both have access to your credit history.

Your goals and objectives should be to get rid of your bad debt so you can put your energy into building up your net worth (assets) instead.

Americans want instant gratification; we like to accumulate "stuff." If you change your strategies, you will charge and buy less stuff and save and invest more.

C H A P T E R 3

Insurance/Risk Management

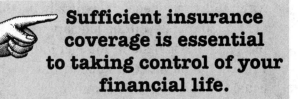

Sufficient insurance coverage is essential to taking control of your financial life.

Often considered a necessary evil, you buy it and hope that you never need it.

There are several types of insurance designed to protect against the risks you encounter in your everyday lives. Here are important facts to consider in choosing a coverage that is right for you and your family.

1. What is life insurance, and what are my life insurance options?

Life insurance is a way to protect your loved ones from loss of income due to your untimely death. It can pay for funeral and burial costs, provide financial resources for your spouse and dependents, and may pay estate tax liabilities.

There are many options to choose from; the right one for you will depend on your need for protection. Let's look at the different types and their basic distinctions:

Term Insurance is designed for one reason-to insure for a set period of time. If you die within the term specified--typically 10, 15, 20 or even 30 years--your beneficiary will receive the cash benefit. Younger individuals who cannot afford cash value insurance usually purchase term insurance.

Cash Value Insurance is insurance where the premium not only pays for insurance protection, but part of it is applied to a cash reserve, which supports the policy in the later years of ownership. An added benefit is that the cash value grows tax-deferred inside the policy. There are three types of cash value insurance:

Whole Life is designed to have a level premium as long as you live, which provides a guaranteed death benefit. It also provides dividends with which additional paid-up insurance can be purchased. Loans can also be made against the cash value of the account, if needed.

Universal Life is a product that combines the protection of a conventional term insurance policy with the current yields available for short-term investments. Unlike whole life, the cash value of a universal life policy grows at a variable rate.

Variable Life, as with whole life and universal life insurance, buys pure insurance protection with a portion of your premium, while the rest is invested by the insurance company on your behalf. You can choose from a variety of investments, and you can choose from straight life insurance that has a fixed premium or universal life, which allows a more flexible premium. You can choose the amount of premiums you can afford to pay.

What should you consider when purchasing life insurance?

Payment for funeral and burial costs.

Providing financial resources for your spouse and dependents.

Covering your estate tax liabilities.

2. Do both parents need life insurance coverage, or should we just insure the breadwinner?

Carrying insurance coverage on both parents is critical in order to make sure there will be coverage to support the care of children should either die prematurely. Even if one parent does not work outside the home, he or she should still have insurance coverage. The parent that is left behind will need the financial resources to take care of living expenses as well as childcare costs and college education.

3. I am in a second marriage, do I have to list my new husband as beneficiary, or can I list my children?

You can choose anyone you want as beneficiary for your life insurance coverage. When deciding, you may want to take into consideration if you will be leaving your new spouse with any financial liabilities should you die prematurely. You should periodically review your beneficiaries on all of your life insurance and annuities, including employer-paid policies.

4. What is long-term care insurance?

Long-term care insurance covers the care needed for individuals with chronic disabilities. This care may be in the individual's home or it may mean custodial care in a nursing home. It isn't restricted just to the elderly; someone who has incurred a debilitating injury may also require long-term care. We

"Every life has value and a need for life insurance"

usually associate long-term care with growing old, and since none of us want to end up in a nursing home facility, we tend to put the decision to purchase long term care on the back burner. As with all insurance, the cost goes up the older you get. The best time to buy is when you are young and healthy-- usually in your fifties.

5. I am single with no children and have prepaid my funeral expenses. Do I need life insurance?

Life insurance is purchased for many reasons like the protection of your loved ones against financial loss upon your death or for the protection of your insurability. It is advisable to buy insurance when you are young and healthy even if you do not have a great need for it now. You may be single and have no children, but that could change. You can purchase insurance that allows you to add additional coverage as your needs change. Talk with your insurance agent, and investigate your available options.

6. How do I determine if I need renters insurance?

You determine if you need renters insurance by adding up the cost of everything in your apartment-- electronics, furniture, clothes, jewelry, etc. If you could not afford to replace all of your personal property, then you will want to consider getting renters insurance. You never realize the value of what you have until you lose it. Also, you may want to assess other liabilities you may have, such as, if someone comes on the property and gets injured because of something of yours.

"Whatever stage of life you are in, insurance is an important part of you overall financial plan."

7. What are some ways to decrease the premiums I pay on my homeowner's and renter's insurance?

To lower your premiums for your home or apartment:

☞ Raise your deductible; the higher the deductible, the larger the discount.

☞ Install a home security system, including a burglar alarm, smoke detectors, carbon monoxide detectors and dead bolt locks.

If you own a newer home, check to see if your rates can be lowered. Sometimes newer homes cost less to insure.

 If you are a senior, check to see if you qualify for a discount.

 Purchase all of your insurance from the same company.

 Shop around and get quotes from several companies.

8. What are some ways to decrease the premiums I pay on my automobile insurance?

• Raise your deductible.

• Cancel the collision coverage or comprehensive coverage if your car is older. (You can put aside the money you save for a down payment on a new car.)

• Purchase all of your insurance from the same company and receive a discount.

• Look for discounts for low-mileage driving, senior citizen, driver training, airbags, garaging your car, anti-theft devices and automatic seat belts.

• Auto clubs, such as AAA, offer discounts, as do some fraternal groups.

9. What is umbrella liability coverage?

Both your homeowner's and your auto insurance policies offer liability coverage. This is important coverage, because if you or yours damage another's property or injure someone, you are liable for the cost of the damages. If you purchase the maximum amount of liability insurance, it will cover $300,000 worth of damages each for property and injury. Sounds like more than enough, right? But what if someone sues you for one million dollars for the pain and suffering he or she has endured due to an automobile accident you caused? Your auto policy would not have the coverage to satisfy the judgment if you were to be sued.

"Be willing to educate yourself, once you learn the value of insurance the decisions will be easy."

An umbrella policy behaves just as you think it might. It will cover you where the other liability coverage ends. Do you need the extra coverage? If you own a large dog that bites or you like to zip through the woods on your snowmobile, or your kids build model rockets, you just may want to consider this extra insurance. A little cost can pay for a lot of peace of mind.

10. How do I know I am paying the lowest amount for my insurance coverage?

There have been many studies showing that individuals pay too much for their insurance coverage. The good news is that the insurance industry is very competitive. Premiums charged for similar coverage will vary drastically. Talking with your insurance agent and carefully shopping and comparing your insurance policy against other policies available to you will insure you are paying fair prices for good coverage.

11. My insurance agent is suggesting I replace my existing insurance, how do I know what to do?

You should first ask "why". Do you truly need a different type of policy or additional coverage or is the agent looking for the commission he or she will receive for the sale? If you trust your agent, listen to their suggestions and make a decision based on their reasoning. If you don't trust them, get a second opinion.

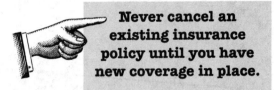

Never cancel an existing insurance policy until you have new coverage in place.

12. We have limited funds. What insurance is most important?

Good question! Every situation will be different. You will have to consider:

- Health Insurance (if not offered by your employer)
- Life Insurance
- Disability Insurance
- Automobile Insurance
- Homeowner or Renter Insurance

Talk with your insurance agent about your biggest, potential liability. Then as money becomes available buy what you need.

Insurance, you hate to pay for it and you do not appreciate it–until you have a loss. You may think you can get by without coverage or very little coverage, but before you decide to take the risk, calculate your assets and determine if you could afford to replace them if they were lost in a fire or stolen. The main idea behind insurance is indemnification, or compensation for a loss. It is used to protect and it is important in your total financial picture.

C H A P T E R   4

Home Ownership

**So, you want to take part in the
"American Dream?"**

I know it is hard to believe, but there are no pros
and cons to owning a home, especially if you
are younger. You have heard that if you're rent-
ing, you're just throwing your money away. Well
that could be true, but maybe not. Buying a
home is a big commitment and may be the
biggest investment you will make. It is a lot of

responsibility, and I hope you will be able to make the best decision for your own situation after you have read this chapter.

1. What are the disadvantages of owning a home?

Maintaining a home takes time and money. Unless you buy a condo with only a flower box in the window, you will have outside maintenance as well as inside maintenance that must be done on a regular basis. Think about it:

Flowers to water ⟶ buy a hose

Lawn to mow ⟶ buy a mower

Leaves to rake ⟶ buy a rake

Snow to shovel ⟶ buy a shovel

Driveway to plow ⟶ buy a plow (yikes)

Repairs to make ⟶ buy a hammer

Home repairs to make? You can save money by doing the repairs yourself, but remember–you still have to buy the tools and equipment to do the job!

46

What about the inside of your new home? More rooms to maintain, more windows to wash, more furniture and appliances to fill those rooms. If you are easily overwhelmed, the stress may not be worth it.

Besides the time and cost, there are other things you may want to consider before deciding to purchase a home. If you think you will be moving out of the area in three years or less, you may not break even on your closing cost. And, of course, you should not be considering buying a home if you are in a rocky marriage, or if you're not in a secure job situation. I do not want to discourage you, but I do want you to know the disadvantages so you can make an educated decision.

2. Okay, so what are the advantages of buying a home?

The best reason I can think of to purchase a home is that you get a

"Owning your own home is the 'American Dream,' but it can also be an 'American Nightmare.' Educate, educate, educate! "

tax deduction for mortgage interest and a deduction for the property taxes you pay. The government came up with these tax breaks several years ago to help stimulate the economy. The good news is that it worked. Over 67% of U. S. households own their homes (with their lenders, of course). In addition to the tax deductions, you get another break when you sell your home. Changes in the tax law now allow you to shelter from capital gains up to $250,000 if you're single and $500,000 if you're married and filing jointly.

It goes without saying that you will have a great feeling of accomplishment when you own your own home, as well as more space. If you purchase your home in an area that is appreciating, it could be one of the best investment decisions you will make.

3. How do I know if I can afford to buy my own home?

It's always better to find out if you can afford something before you begin seriously shopping. And with mortgage rates being low and home prices going up, many people are wondering if they should buy their first home now. So how do your determine if you can afford to buy?

Answers to a couple of questions can help you decide.

First, do you have enough savings to get into a home? How much would it take? Affording a home means more than having enough cash for a down payment.

Second, can you afford the regular, ongoing monthly expenses? You'll also need some cash for some of the expenses that come with a first home. Things like a lawnmower, ladder and basic lawn implements. Home centers love first-time homeowners! Create a "make believe" budget that includes a house payment. Don't forget to include taxes, insurance and some money each month for home repairs.

"For many, home owner-ship is a sign of success and status. Be sure to purchase a home for the right reasons."

"Often overlooked: Property should be surveyed to avoid bound-ary disputes."

Do your "homework" and make an educated decision.

4. What is pre-approval?

If you are very serious about buying a home, you can get pre-approved for a mortgage. This will show the sellers that you are serious, and if there is more than one offer on the home you want to buy, you will have an advantage because you know and they know that you can get the money. Caution--pre-qualified is not the same as pre-approved. To get pre-approved, you need to sit down with a mortgage lender, fill out all of the paperwork, and provide them with all of the information necessary to give you a thumbs up for the amount of money you would like to borrow. Usually this pre-approval is good for a certain period of time. If you do not get a home within that time frame, you will need to get approved again. Be sure to ask your lender how long the pre-approval is good.

5. If I find the home of my dreams, are there any other considerations I should take into account?

Yes. The decision to buy a particular home depends on three areas:

Location, Location, Location. Is the home's location convenient to work, shopping, schools and recreation? Is the area appreciating, and how much are the property taxes? Is it a high crime area? How good is the school district?

The type of home you purchase needs to fit your lifestyle. If you travel or are not home a lot, you might want to look at something low maintenance, like a condo. There is a lot of variety to choose from--traditional, condominiums or multifamily units. The good news is you have plenty of choices.

How much home can you afford? The amount of down payment and closing costs you will have to accumulate depends upon how much house you can afford. The following three rules should help you get an idea of how large a mortgage you can carry.

1. Your monthly mortgage payment should not exceed more than one and a half week's worth of take-home pay.

2. Your monthly mortgage payment should not exceed 28% of your gross monthly income.

"You do not have to buy the biggest, most expensive home, but look for the right home for you. Some say you should look for the least expensive home in your neighborhood and move up from there."

3. Your total monthly debt obligations including the mortgage should not exceed 35% your gross monthly income.

6. What are the types of mortgages to choose from?

There are several common types of mortgages:

30-year fixed rate mortgage is the standard and probably the most popular. While an adjustable mortgage may offer a lower interest rate at first, most home buyers opt for fixed-rate mortgages for the security of knowing that the monthly payments will never change and that they will be lower than those of a 15-year mortgage.

15-year fixed rate. Your monthly payments will be higher if you take out a 15-year fixed-rate mortgage, but the total interest you pay out over the life of the loan will be substantially lower. A 15-year fixed-rate mortgage is a good idea if you can afford the higher payments. Want to turn your 30-year mortgage into a 15-year mortgage at no cost? It's easy. Just make sufficient additional principal payments each month on your 30-year mortgage so that it will be paid off over the shorter period of time. You also can cut your repayment period down by taking out a biweekly mortgage, which means you make the equivalent of one extra payment each year.

Adjustable-rate mortgages are types of mortgages that offer extremely low rates that are subject to change. Many have a limit or ceiling as to how high their interest rate can go and a limit or floor to how low they can go. The attraction of adjustable rate mortgages is their low initial rate, but the danger is that the low rate may be left in the dust by rising interest rates. If you're contemplating staying in your new home for less than five years, then an adjustable-rate mortgage may be the best choice for you.

7. What other costs can I expect when I purchase a home?

Closing cost take most first time home buyers by surprise. By now, you know that surprise is an element that will work against successful financial planning. The following closing costs account for most of what you can expect when buying a home.

Be aware that additional fees incurred when purchasing a home can really stack up!

Mortgage Application Fee
Depending on your lender, this expense can run from no cost to several hundred dollars.

Origination Fee
This is the fee that a mortgage department or company charges to process your loan.

Private Mortgage Insurance Fee
If you don't have a 20% down payment but are still a candidate for a mortgage, you may be required to insure that the difference between your down payment and the 20% figure can be paid.

Appraisal Fee
You pay a professional to assess the market value of your desired home for the bank. Such fees start at $200, with no ceiling.

Home Inspection Fee
This fee is around $200 and pays a professional to inspect the house for defects. If you don't do this, you might end up with substantially less than you bargained for.

Credit Report Fee
This is paid to the bank to run your credit report to check how creditworthy you are.

Attorney Fee

You will need to pay your attorney to check the purchase contract and mortgage agreement, usually a flat fee paid based on the law firm you use.

Bank Attorney Fee

This pays the cost of the bank's legal work.

Points

Most lenders charge one or two points at closing--typically 1% to 3% of the loan. Each point equals 1% of the loan amount, so two points on a $125,000 mortgage would be $2,500. The problem with points is that they often pose a problem for homebuyers trying to compare mortgage terms. The impact of points on total carrying costs compounds the confusion. How much this affects the effective annual rate of the loan depends on how long you intend to own the house. The significance of points diminishes as the period of time you own the home increases.

"It has long been the dream of Americans to own their own homes. With proper planning, you too can realize that dream."

8. I have a lot of equity in my home and could use the money for credit card debt payments. Is that a good use of the equity?

Sometimes it makes sense to take part of the equity in your home, but the penalty of misusing the money will stay with you for a very long time. Here are some reasons to take out a home equity loan:

To pay for home repairs or remodeling.

To combine and pay off credit card debt.

To purchase a new car.

For emergency purposes, you can have a home equity line of credit.

9. My parents have been advised to do a reverse mortgage on their home. What is it, and should they do it?

That is a tricky question. First, reverse mortgage is an arrangement where a homeowner will borrow money against the equity of their home and receive regular payments (tax free) from the lender until the balance reaches the credit limit of equity. The mortgages are available with the Federal Housing Administration (FHA). When the money reaches the credit limit of the equity, the lender gets repayment in a lump sum or the house. As you can see, there is some merit to taking out a reverse mortgage, but I feel it should be a last resort. You would not want your parents to lose their home. My advice would be to seek expert advice. In fact, you are required to attend a free counseling session before you apply, and by doing this you can address the pros and cons.

10. New home versus used– which should I buy?

Good question and one asked all of the time. This is a hard question to answer, and everyone you talk with will have a different opinion. This decision usually has nothing to do with money and everything to do with personal taste.

One of the fundamental mistakes that consumers make is a rush to judgment. They often dismiss a new home or a resale when one is far more appropriate for them than the other. So how do you decide which best fits your needs and personality?

"Used, new, house, condo. Whatever you decide to buy, it will be one of the smartest decisions you make."

**Below are a few pros and cons
in the new-resale debate:**

Locale: The most said real estate mantra,
"location, location, location," is still relevant.
Most older, established neighborhoods are in
the town's center, which can be good or bad
depending on the vitality of your urban area.
New subdivisions -- and newer schools -- are
generally on the outskirts. But the expense of a
daily commute is one factor that many buyers
forget to consider.

Price: Existing homes are usually less expensive
per square foot, in part because of escalating
land costs in new subdivisions. But ownership
costs are considered more predictable -- almost
inevitable -- in a new home, especially considering the cost of a code upgrade or remodeling

of a vintage home. Some builders will include closing costs as part of their price of a new home, although that builder has a set amount he or she must get from that home in order to make a profit. Price is more readily negotiable for an existing home. Do your homework.

Move-in complications, advantages: The resale is sitting there waiting for occupancy, warts and all. The wait for a new home can seem interminable, though the buyer can check on quality control as it's being built. If your finished house is among the first in a new subdivision, prepare to navigate through construction teams and precariously misplaced nails for months on end. And don't forget that daytime hammer serenade.

Neighborhood: People moving into new neighborhoods are more homogeneous -- the same things that appeal to you also appeal to others like you. When a development goes up, it offers an opportunity for you to help create your own neighborhood lifestyle. If you want to move into a community where your children have lots of playmates, that may be for you. In an older community, people have moved in and out over the years, and you tend to have more diverse neighbors, including older people, singles, families and renters.

Living space and design: Lower building costs of the past mean more home for the money for the buyer of a resale. Resale basements may have been finished out nicely for additional living space. On the other hand, new-construction homes often employ more efficient, innovative uses of square footage and property.

Customization: In a new house, you can pick your own color schemes, flooring, kitchen cabinets, appliances, custom wiring for TVs, computers, phones, speakers, etc., as well as have more upgrade options. In a used home, you rely largely on the previous resident's tastes and technological whims.

Character: While many new homes are built in "contextual" style, which blends elements of the old and the new, it's still hard to emulate a pre-Civil War house in New Orleans, a Victorian home in San Francisco or a brick Row House in Boston. Hardwood floors, vaulted windows, high ceilings, built-in cabinetry and other design nuances express a certain individuality in older homes that's nearly impossible to copy. Many new-home buyers believe they put the character in their own homes.

Safety: Builders have to follow very strict guide-lines in new homes and additions, especially in the West and Northwest, where earthquake safety standards must be observed. In general, new homes are usually more fire-safe and better accommodating of new security and garage-door systems.

Landscaping: Mature trees, robust shrubs, gardens, rose bushes and perennially well-watered lawns are some of the rewards of an older home, while most new homes are apt to yield wee trees, fewer walkways and sparse vegetation. Landscaping is an expensive proposition today for the cost-conscious home builder.

Energy efficiency: Advantage: new construction. Game, set and match as well. New-home designers can use new building materials such as glazed Energy Star windows, thicker insulation and other technology that will lower future energy costs for the owner. Most states now have minimum energy-efficiency requirements for new construction. Kitchens and laundry areas in new homes are designed to house more efficient energy-saving appliances. Older homes, unless they have undergone an energy retrofit, usually cost much more per square foot to air-condition and heat.

Amenities: Many new subdivisions offer neighborhood clubhouses, swimming pools, playgrounds, bike and jogging trails and picnic venues for residents. Older homes don't, although many have better access to urban shopping venues and restaurants because they're part of old, self-containing city-planning philosophies.

Maintenance: The charm of an older home often goes hand in hand with increased maintenance, especially if the previous owner(s) were not vigilant in upkeep. Building materials may be harder to replace or match in an expansion or remodeling. New homes generally come with at least a one-year warranty for the repair of some problems that develop as they settle into their foundation. But know what your warranty covers. Many are elusively written.

Taxes: Newer homes tend to spring up in less-developed, outlying municipalities, which may impose higher taxes because they're subsidizing fewer inhabitants than the central metropolitan area. Your community will still need fire and police coverage, sidewalks, sewers and probably a new school. A more established home in a built-out area has a little more predictable tax structure. Increasingly, "new" is no longer an option in some towns, and neither is "old" for most folks there.

Compromise is obviously the name of the new-

or-resale home-buying game, as it becomes apparent that the perfect house and perfect site probably don't really exist. And finding what you want can be a result of doing your homework. Whether buying a new or resale home, always hire a properly credentialed individual to inspect the premises before you settle.

11. How can I get the most out of my home when I sell it?

Here are some tips to follow to successfully sell your home:

1. Make room. Clear out as much furniture as you can. Put it in storage, give it to Goodwill or have a garage sale.

2. Follow your nose. A home should smell good. That means no noticeable odor -- no pet scent, no stale cooking smells and no cigarette smoke.

3. Remember--the next buyer is as lazy as you are. If the property needs work (dated wallpaper, ratty carpet), have it replaced now so that all buyers have to picture is moving day.

4. Do the baby test. Does your potential market include families with young kids? If so, ask yourself, would I put my child down on this floor to crawl around the room? If not, you  know what you have to fix. Likewise, if your walls sport grimy smudges or handprints, it might be worth it to paint.

5. Make your home ageless. There's a difference between an old house and a classic home. If the house looks 40 years old with 40-year-old paint, 40-year-old appliances and 40-year-old carpet, that's a hard sell. Keep everything fresh and up-to-date and you have a solid home in an established neighborhood -- a real looker.

12. I am in my late forties and am thinking of purchasing a home. Am I too old?

You are never too old and it's never too late to purchase a home if you have read the above questions and are willing to accept the responsibilities that come with owning your own home.

CHAPTER 5

Investments

At some point in your life, you will want to consider how you might start investing for those long-term goals you have set for yourself. Saving for a longer period of time is often referred to as investing.

There are several types of investments, and determining your financial goals is the first step in finding the right kind for you. Saving for a down payment on a house is different than investing for your child's college, which is also different from investing for your retirement. Your financial goals will help you determine what type of investment accounts you want to have.

The sooner you set your goals and begin striving to achieve them, the better off you will be.

1. What are the ways you can invest?

Actually, there are two ways to invest. You can invest by lending your money. When you loan someone your money, such as a bank, a form of government, or a corporation, you will receive a promise that it will repay you with interest. Interest is the payment for the use of your money.

You can also purchase or own an asset. Your hope is that it will appreciate over time. While owning the asset, you may receive dividends or other distributions from certain types of investments.

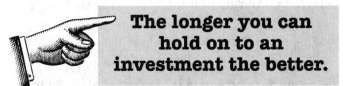

The longer you can hold on to an investment the better.

2. Why is it important to invest in tax deferred investments?

Tax-advantaged accounts can help you accumulate wealth to meet some financial goals. Traditional and Roth IRA accounts are structured for retirement savings, as is a 401(k) or 403(b) retirement plan.

First things first. If your employer offers a 401(k) plan where they match all or part of your contributions to the plan, then that's where you should start investing for retirement. Contribute up to the limit of the employer match before considering opening a different type of retirement account. From there you could consider a Roth or Traditional IRA account. With a Roth IRA you are investing after-tax dollars, but qualified distributions out of the account are tax-free in retirement. With a Traditional IRA, contributions are made with pre-tax dollars but qualified distributions are taxed at your ordinary income tax rate in retirement. If you're saving for your children's college expenses then Section 529 college savings plans, prepaid tuition plans, Coverdell Education Savings Accounts (formerly called education IRAs) and U.S. savings bonds can provide tax-advantaged investments for college expenses.

3. If I take advantage of my company's investments, how do I know what to choose that will be best for me?

If you're investing in a 401(k) it's likely that you'll have to choose among a list of investments provided by the plan administrator. You'll make the best choice that you can from the investments on the list. Have your plan administrator explain the investment choices. Pay careful attention to the annual expense ratios and any sales loads (commissions) on the funds. You'll select a stock-bond-cash allocation based on your choice of investments. People new to investing are best served by buying no-load, indexed mutual funds. You aren't going to beat the market by buying an index fund -- you're going to match the performance of the market index. Index funds typically have much lower annual expense ratios than actively managed funds, keeping more of the investment return in your account. There are stock and bond index mutual funds, or you can choose a hybrid fund that invests in both stocks and bonds.

4. Then why would I want to invest in taxable accounts?

Taxable accounts are for your current financial requirements, and for short-term financial goals, like a down payment on a car or home. There are some exceptions to that, like the first-time homeowner provisions in IRA accounts. But for the most part, taxable accounts best meet your need for short-term goals and liquid-ity. Speaking of liquidity needs, most financial planners will recommend that you have three to six months worth of living expenses in an account that you can access without penalty. If you haven't built up an emergency fund, here's where you should start investing. Buy short-term, money market investments in taxable accounts.

5. What are my options for investing?

Once you've decided on taxable vs. tax-advantage accounts, it's time to decide what to buy as investments in the accounts.

What to Buy

When people buy financial investments, they choose between stocks, bonds and cash.

Cash is where you will put your short-term money. Some examples are savings accounts or money market accounts. These invest-ments mature in a year or less. They usually pay a low interest, but are liquid.

Bonds or fixed-income investments will mature more than a year from now. Bonds are called fixed-income

"It is a fact that everyone has an opinion about the right investment strategy. The truth is we all will prosper with strategies based on our specific goals and objectives."

investments because the returns on the investment are contractual. The interest payments on a bond comprise the fixed-income component of the bond's investment return. Short-term CDs can be considered money market investments while longer-term CDs fall in the bond camp.

Stocks are a way you can buy a fractional ownership interest in a company. Stock returns aren't contractual, since their return on investment is based on the company's earnings. Stock investors take on a higher level of volatility (risk) in the stock's return and because of that higher level of risk expect higher average returns -- which they may not realize.

6. What is risk?

Fortunately or unfortunately, for many people risk has an adverse meaning. Some may think they are just conservative and feel they should not risk their hard-earned money. Others feel that they must take risks no matter what.

The true answer is if you take no risks with your investments, you typically will not earn a high enough return to achieve your financial goals. But if you take too many risks, you may not be able to sleep at night. The further away you are from the needs to use the money, the more risk you will be able to take.

Are your willing to ride the up's and down's of the stock market? How much risk are you willing to take?

"The market will fluctuate up and down-- that is a guarantee. There is no guarantee that you will not lose your money, so invest wisely."

In general, financial markets price investments on the notion that the more risk to the investor, the higher the return that the investor will expect on the investment. An investor's attitude toward risk will influence their mix of cash, stock and bond investments. Many long-term investors invest too conservatively. To reach your financial goals you need to see the purchasing power of your investment portfolio increase over time. Your investment returns have to keep pace with inflation to maintain the portfolio's purchasing power and outpace inflation to increase its power.

The further away your investment goals, the more willing you should be to invest in stocks. The closer your goals, the more money you should have invested in cash.

7. I have heard that there are different kinds of risks to consider. What are they?

There are several different risks to consider. Here are the seven most important:

1. *Business Risk* - Refers to the inability of some companies to maintain their competitive positions and earnings growth.

2. *Market Risk* - Refers to the possibility of an adverse price change.

3. *Money Rate Risk* - Refers to the risk of change in the price of a fixed income security resulting from a change in the interest paid on securities currently being issued.

4. *Purchasing Power Risk* - Refers to the risk of loss in income and principal because inflation decreases the purchasing power of the dollar.

5. *Investment Risk* – is the risk that the value of your investment will go down.

6. *Inflation Risk* – is something that not many people think about, but consider this: Inflation reduces the purchasing power of your money, meaning you won't be able to buy as much in the future as you can today with the same amount of money.

7. *Interest Rate Risk* – is a risk that your investment's value will fluctuate with changes in the general level in interest rates.

If you take no risks with your investments, you typically will not earn a high enough return to achieve your financial goals.

8. How do I allocate my assets to various investments?

A strategy called asset allocation is the process of dividing investment assets among different types of options such as stocks, bonds, mutual funds, cash and other kinds of securities investments. As investors, we don't normally pay a lot of attention to asset allocation. We need to realize that it's the key decision that determines investment success, not how successful you were at picking stocks or mutual funds. The process of asset allocation may include one or all of the following approaches:

Strategic Asset Allocation - Uses historical data (mean rates of return and standard deviations) in an attempt to understand how the asset has performed and is likely to perform over long periods of time. The goal is not to "beat" the market, but to establish a long-term investment strategy using a core mix of assets.

Tactical Asset Allocation - Uses periodic assumptions regarding the performance and characteristics of the asset and/or the economy. This approach attempts to improve portfolio performance by making "mid-course" changes in the long-term strategy based on near-term expectations.

Finding the right allocation mix for your investments can be a balancing act. Depending on your tolerance for risk, your age and the amount you can invest the balance can fluctuate.

Dynamic Asset Allocation - Involves changes in investor circumstances, which may lead to the modification of policies, objectives and/or risk tolerances. Resulting changes are intended to maintain equilibrium between the investor's policies & objectives and the asset allocation process.

9. How do I know what to do?

Start studying; a little knowledge can go a long way. You don't need a doctoral degree in economics to invest wisely and well. But you will need to bring yourself up to speed on some of the most prevalent factors that shape the markets in which you're investing. Doing so requires a basic understanding of how economies (ours and others') work to shape the various markets in which investment opportunities are available.

"If you place your money in a venue that does not move up and down with the market, it is not an investment, it is a savings account."

10. I have heard a lot about diversification. What does it mean?

There are no foolproof investment strategies -- but there are several strategies that have proven to be reliable and successful. One of the best is diversification. No matter what, diversification can work in your favor. What is it? Simply put, it's the division of your assets into several different types of investments. The theory being that when one investment is slipping from favor, another is often gaining ground.

11. What is dollar cost averaging?

Dollar cost averaging is designed to reduce the volatility of your investments. When regularly purchasing or selling investments such as stocks or mutual funds, the most difficult thing is the ability to "time" the market. Using the strategy of dollar cost averaging avoids this. Typically stocks and bonds or mutual funds are purchased in a fixed dollar amount at regular intervals, regardless of what direction the market is moving. The purchases when made are averaged whether the market is up or down.

12. How do I pick a financial advisor, and what questions do I ask?

There are many questions to ask an advisor when you interview them:

What is your education background?

How long have you been in the financial industry?

How are you compensated for your services?

What products and services do you provide?

Another great way to find the right financial planner is to ask your family, friends and associates who they work with and if they are happy with them. Get several names and interview them for the best fit for your needs.

The bottom line is it is easy not to plan ahead. For many, concerns about investing take a back seat to current realities of purchasing a new home and raising children. But by the time they reach their 40's the need to invest starts to set in. The reality is the sooner you start the better. A careful analysis of your goals and objectives will determine how much you actually will need.

C H A P T E R 6

Retirement

Modern retirement is not a simple matter.

It cannot be successful without planning, motivating and adjusting as circumstances and conditions change. So often, retirement planning is based on assumptions--you assume you will retire at a certain age, with a certain income and live to a certain age.

Your life deserves the best thought you can give it, and you will need to educate, motivate and pay attention to your particular circumstances.

1. I do not have any money. How can I plan for retirement?

A common mistake people make is that they think they need to have money to have a retirement plan. Actually, you need to have the plan in place so that when you have a positive cash flow you will be able to direct the money toward your retirement.

2. When should I start planning for retirement?

My advice is to start saving for retirement when you get your first job, and make use of the qualified plan that your employers offer allowing you to put away money pre-tax. The time to start planning for retirement is now. It is never too early or too late to start planning. The longer you wait to get started, the more money you will need. Once you have an idea of how and when you want to retire you will then be able to estimate your expenses.

3. How will I know if I am saving enough money?

When you estimate your purchasing power of your investments for retirement, you estimate it in current dollars and then in future, inflated dollars. Here's a helpful rule of thumb: To maintain the same standard of living in retirement that you enjoy today, you will probably need an annual retirement income of approximately 75 to 85 percent of the amount you spend today. You need to prepare a detailed retirement expense budget and revisit it every year.

"It is never too early or too late to start planning for your retirement."

4. I want to retire early. Is it possible?

Well, whether you choose to retire early or it's forced upon you, you will need to take a hard look at how you will be able to meet your current living expenses when you retire, and also 10, 20 and 30 or more years down the road. It is

"Having a trusted financial advisor working with you to plan for retirement is the wisest decision you will make."

Want to retire early? Planning ahead will ensure you have the financial resources to enjoy the rest of your life.

possible to retire early and retire well, but you will need to be certain that your long-term financial security is assured. If you have accumulated sufficient personal resources, your projections may indeed show that you can afford to retire early.

5. What are the best ways to save for retirement?

Check with the benefits department of your company to find out what your employer offers. If you work in the public sector as a teacher, or as a state or city employee, you will have either a 403(b) or a 457 plan available.

The earlier you begin to save and the longer you have until retirement, the less you will need to save.

6. What is a defined contribution plan?

With a defined contribution plan, your employer makes a certain contribution to the pension fund each and every year. Contributions are based on salary and years of service. At retirement, you will receive a pension benefit or lump-sum payment based on what-ever happens to be in the fund at the time. This type of plan is usually very advantageous if you have a long working life and if your employer contributes enough to build up a substantial retirement fund.

7. What is a defined benefit pension plan?

This plan is provided by your employer and is structured to gen-erate a certain predetermined annual retirement benefit. The amount is usually based on final or highest salaries and years of serv-ice. Depending on your employer, the benefit calculations will differ. Information can be found in your employee handbook.

8. My employer is offering a 401(k) plan. Should I participate?

Participating in the 401(k) plan your employer offers may be the single best decision you make to

"Every day puts you one-step closer; don't let retirement sneak up on you."

accumulate retirement dollars. These plans are sometimes referred to salary-reduction plans, because you put part of your salary into an investment account with an investment company that your company chooses. The contributions are tax deductible and grow tax deferred. Many employers will match their employees' contributions (i.e. 25 to 50 cents to the account for every dollar the employee contributes). Think of it as "free money."

Let's see...tax deduction, tax deferral and free money.

The answer is yes.

You should participate in your company's 401(k) plan.

9. I'm married. Why should I worry about retirement? My husband will take care of me, right?

You should be able to take care of yourself. It is wonderful that you have someone to take care of you, but what if you lose his support through death or divorce? And even if you grow old together, women outlive men by an average of five years. So understanding what your retirements needs are and the products available to you will insure that you will make the right retirement decisions for yourself if or when you end up alone.

10. What should I be considering when I determine my retirement income?

There are many calculators available either online or through your financial advisor to determine living expenses after retirement. Will you own your home? If you've paid off your home, will your expenses decrease?

"Retirement planning is based on assumptions-- you assume a retirement age, income and life expectancy. You know what they say about assumptions, don't you?"

Will you still have health insurance provided in retirement, or will you have to find your own?

What will your lifestyle look like in retirement? Will you be staying at home sitting on your rocking chair or traveling?

Will you live the life of leisure, or do you plan on working part-time or starting that business you always wanted?

As you can see, the type of lifestyle you "plan" will depend on the nest egg you will need to accumulate.

11. Can I expect Social Security to be available to me when I retire?

If you have contributed to Social Security for the minimum length of time, full benefits will begin upon retirement at age 65, or reduced benefits at age 62. People born in 1960 or later will receive their full benefits at age 67. I feel the age to receive benefits will continue to move later as more are paid out to the millions of baby boomers moving toward retirement. You should not count on Social Security as being the only source of income in retirement, and it will not be enough to ensure a continuation of the lifestyle you have planned. If you work for the federal, state or local government and/or non-profit organizations, you may be eligible for pensions based on earnings not covered by Social Security. Your benefits will come from the Federal Employee Retirement System or the Public Employees Retirement System.

12. Are there things to consider regarding Social Security?

Here are four myths about Social Security you need to know:

Social Security Myth #1

It's in the Constitution. Social Security is not included in the United States Constitution. It was a part of the Great Depression's New Deal package of programs that President Franklin D. Roosevelt and his advisors conceived and presented to Congress. Their goal was to give America's hard working people "something to live on when they are old and have stopped working." Congress passed it in 1935.

Social Security Myth #2

An Account with Your Name on It. Many people believe the money taken from their paychecks for Social Security taxes (FICA) is placed in an account with their name on it. This account then becomes the source of their future benefits, like an IRA or other genuine retirement account. That is a myth. Social Security is an inter-generational program, meaning that today's workers support today's retirees. In 1945, there were 41.9 workers per beneficiary.

Today there are only 3.4 workers supporting each beneficiary and the Social Security Administration projects that the ratio will slowly decline to a mere 1.9 workers by 2075. It is this decrease in the ratio, as well as the fact that our seniors are living longer, that is going to have the greatest impact on Social Security's insolvency in the future, unless significant changes are implemented. Here is the bottom line. There is no account with your name on it collecting real interest, and there is no guarantee that when you reach retirement age the generation under you will be contributing enough to support your retirement benefits.

Social Security Myth #3

The Trust Funds. The Social Security taxes we pay today are funding the benefits of today's retirees. Currently, more money is coming into the system than is being paid out; hence, there is a surplus. Logically, one would expect that those surplus monies are being saved for the future in trust funds just like you would save money in an IRA or other account to later take out and fund retirement. But that is yet another myth. In reality, the trust funds are comprised of IOUs which the federal government leaves in return for borrowing that money each year to reduce the federal deficit (or for a couple of years in the 90s, to show a surplus). But beginning in an estimated 14 years, when those trust funds need to be tapped to start paying benefits to baby boomers, where is the money going to come from to pay the interest on and eventually redeem those IOUs? According to the Social Security Administration, the options are: "increased taxation, increased borrowing (i.e., the sale of more U.S. Treasury bonds to the public) and/or a reduction in other government expenditures." Other sources suggest a fourth option not mentioned above: a reduction in benefits to future retirees.

Social Security Myth #4

Full Benefits at 65. A fourth myth is that you will be able to retire and collect full social security benefits at age 65. Although most people don't realize it, the rules changed twenty years ago. Everyone born from 1943 to 1954 will have to wait until age 66 to collect full benefits, while those born 1960 or later must wait until they turn 67. Currently, workers can choose to start collecting their benefits at age 62, but they receive only 80 percent of what they would get if they waited until 65. In the future, that decreases even more. Those born in

1960 or later who choose to start collecting Social Security at age 62 will receive only 70 percent of what they would get if they waited until age 67.

The Impact on Your Future

Myth #1 is an interesting fact, but not something you need to worry about. Expect Social Security to be around for a long time, even if it's not guaranteed by the U.S. Constitution. But Myths #2, #3 and #4 are cause for concern. You may have learned that your Social Security benefits are not set aside and reserved in your name, but will depend on the generations under you. That group will not be large enough to support you in the same manner that our seniors are being supported today. But most importantly, you should now be aware that your Social Security benefits might be less than you expect. The question for most of us is this: Can we depend on Social Security to provide significant financial support in our retirement like it is for today's retirees? The answer depends on whether or not you believe the trust funds will be there for you.

Retirement planning is very important. Even if you are struggling to raise a family, plan for retirement now. Retirement can be very pleasant if plans are well thought out in advance. Write down your retirement desires, needs and wants. It's not too soon. Know where you want to live, how you want live, if and when you want to make a move and why. Never make hasty decisions about such an important issue.

If you own your home, make sure that all expensive electrical appliances, i.e. stove, fridge, freezer, washer, dryer, computer are replaced before retirement. Have all major house repairs done.

"The future is going to look exactly the way you plan it. Draw those plans carefully."

The time to pay off all of your debts is BEFORE you retire. This will allow you more peace of mind when you are living on a fixed income.

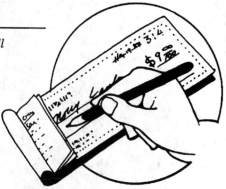

Retire with no debt. Pay off all credit cards, your mortgage, your car and any other outstanding loans. Replacing your vehicle will be the biggest post-work expense. Have enough money in the bank to do this.

Use credit cards or line-of-credit for major expenses only if you can pay the balance at the end of each month. Try to pay everything with cash. Begin to track your expenses to give an accurate picture of spending habits.

 **Lose the bad habits, expand on the good.**

CHAPTER 7

Kids & Money

You may say that Kids and Money is a big oxymoron. If you have kids, you probably do not think you can have money. We want our children to have good money habits and make good money decisions. Unless parents take the time to discuss finances, the family budget and the proper use of money, children will not have the opportunity to get the best financial education. Sad but true--our children usually get their financial information from their friends. But where do their friends get their information? This section of the book addresses how to raise money savvy children and pay for their education, and is written for you to share with your children and grandchildren.

1. When do I start talking with my children about money?

As with all financial education, it can never be too early to start teaching your children about money. Of course when they are young, simple references to money and savings is best. For example, purchase a fun bank-- something that makes a noise or does something cute when you put money into it. If it will get them to laugh or smile they will develop good feelings about saving.

2. Once their money is saved in their bank, should I start an investment program?

Yes, yes, yes. Did I say yes? Now having said yes, let me qualify my answer. A trip to the bank to open a savings account is a good way to show how the process works. An interest bearing savings account at your bank is a great place to put short-term money. If you are saving money for long term goals, your choices will be different.

3. My child is asking for an allowance. Is this a good idea, and how much is appropriate?

An allowance is good for teaching your children money skills. There are a lot of different opinions as to what age to start giving allowance and what the criteria should be for receiving it. Here are some ways to get started:

1. Start when your child is young, usually when they start asking you to buy them things at the store.

2. Put the amount you give them into your budget spreadsheet so it will not be a strain on your cash flow.

3. Decide right from the start if the allowance will be based on your child doing certain tasks to receive it.

4. Decide if there will be restrictions on what your child can do with the money right from the start.

"How your child sees you manage your money will be remembered more than what you say to them about managing their money."

5. If the rules change when your child gets older, be sure to sit down with them and let them have their say.

6. Decide if their allowance will be linked to their behavior.

4. Should I let my child get a job? Won't it interfere with their studies?

Good question. If their work income is necessary for the family's cash flow, the rules change. That money will go into the income section of the family budget and be used for everyday expenses. If they do not have to work but want to make their own money, again you will need to sit down with them to discuss the rules. Here are some questions to consider:

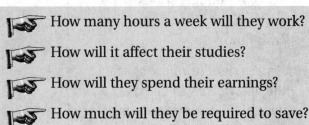

☞ How many hours a week will they work?

☞ How will it affect their studies?

☞ How will they spend their earnings?

☞ How much will they be required to save?

Also, be aware of the child labor laws. Contact the Ohio Department of Commerce, Wage and Hour Bureau in your area for more information

5. How much should they be required to save?

I am certain there are different views. When my children started to work, they had to save 50% of what they earned, and the balance was theirs to spend. I also required them to help with larger items, such as expensive clothing, tennis shoes, stereo equipment, etc. With the money they saved, they were able to purchase their first cars, help with insurance and help pay for their education. I felt they would appreciate what they had more if they helped pay into it.

6. I would like to start an account for my child's education. How do I get started?

A great plan for savings can start even before your child is born. Start by putting any extra cash in an account; every little bit helps. After your child is born, save "all" of the money they receive as gifts-- Christmas, birthdays, etc.

"Remember, the more financially savvy your children are raised, the more likely they will have the money to take care of themselves when grown, and less likely to need your financial help."

7. What type of account should I use?

There are many options available to you for college savings:

• *The 529 Savings Plan* is a great way to save for college. Every state has its own investment product, and these plans provide state and federal tax breaks. Money you put into these accounts is tax-free and can be used for a variety of educational costs.

Over 12 years, the money earned from good grade cards and its interest can make a nice nest egg for college expenses.

• *The "Lifetime Learning Credit"* and *"Hope Credit"* are also ways to invest for post secondary education by taking advantage of federal income tax credits.

8. What is the Tuition Trust Authority Plan?

Some states have Tuition Trust Authority plans that offer affordable ways to help save for higher education through a guaranteed savings fund,

102

which gives families more control over their investments. Large mutual fund companies usually manage these investments. To find out if you can utilize the plan in your state, check with your State Trust Authority for its requirements.

9. What is the cost of college today, and how will I know what my child will need for college?

The average cost of a college education in 2003 was:

Community College
(2-year associate degree)

Tuition and fees............ $5,500

Public University
(4-year bachelors degree)

Tuition and fees............ $29,200
Room and board $23,190

Private University
(4-year bachelors degree)

Tuition and fees............ $81,504
Room and board $31,130

"It is important in any wealth accumulation program to involve the people around you, children included. Communication is the key to success."

These averages will change every year, so my advice to you is run your figures every year and apply an inflation factor. College will be a big expense, so an early start to saving is very important.

10. I don't think I will have enough saved for college. What types of grants are out there to supplement what we have saved?

There are billions of dollars of assistance available to you and your child to help offset the costs of college. Here are the most recognized:

Federal Pell Grants are given if you are a low-income family. The most you can borrow is $4,000 per student based on need, but this amount changes each year.

The Federal Supplemental Educational Opportunity Grant is administered by universities and offers aid from $100 to $4,000 per student per year.

Federal Work Study is a program that provides part-time work for the student during the school year and is often required by the university if they have grant assistance.

11. If my child does not qualify for a grant, what loans are there for us to consider?

Education loans are available typically as need-based to help families fill the gap when they do not have the funds, but also as non need-based to support the family with assets but not enough cash for college. Unfortunately, loans are the only option open to most students and parents.

Perkins loans are loaned specifically to the student, and parents are not required to co-sign. Repayments start nine months after graduation and will need to be paid back over a ten year period.

Stafford loans are variable and have an interest rate limit of 8.25% (subject to change). The qualifications are not need-based, and these loans are awarded to most students who apply. Unlike Perkins, interest accumulates immediately, but payment can still be postponed until graduation.

Plus loans (Parents Loans for Undergraduate Students) are also non-needs-based loans, where the recipient is the parent and not the student. These loans can be for the entire annual cost of college minus any financial aid received. They have a variable interest rate, and payments start in sixty days but from graduation and can be spread over ten years like the Perkins Loan.

Private Loans, such as home equity lines of credit, bank lines of credit or personal loans, will be another choice for you. The downside to these loans is that the payments start immediately and the interest is normally higher.

12. What is the "Rule of 72," and how does it affect college savings?

This rule is important with any investments. Here is how it works: Your money will double over a certain number of years, depending on interest rates or investment returns. For example, divide your return into the number 72 if you expect to get an 8 percent interest rate. 72 divided by 8 is 9. So, your investment will double in 9 years, hence the Rule of 72.

Since you typically have many years to save and invest for your child, a $100 monthly investment averaging 8 percent will be $48,000 in 18 years.

In America today, close to 90 percent of families find it difficult to sit down and discuss money issues. What is surprising to me is that we expect our children to be good with their money, but fail to recognize that they will connect their childhood experiences with how we as parents deal with our own money. How you handle money will just reinforce how your children will handle it now and as adults. If you struggle with money, so will your children. If you do not take the time to sit down with your children and discuss budgeting, saving and spending, they will grow up and proceed to make terrible money mistakes.

Your college saving strategies should be:

- Start early.

- Be aggressive.

- Evaluate often.

- Check out tax advantaged investment choices.

- Set your goals and objectives, and reevaluate every year.

- Reallocate your investments to less risky choices as your time frame shortens.

- Investigate your grant, scholarship and loan options.

CHAPTER 8

Identity Theft

Sad but true--you are at risk everyday to have your identity stolen. This type of white-collar crime has become more and more popular over the years.

When someone steals your identity, you have serious problems. Suddenly, you're on the defensive in that job interview, rental application, or loan approval you thought would be a breeze.

Unfortunately, you might not know that the identity theft has happened until it's too late. The thief, armed with just a few pieces of information--credit card number, social security number, driver's license number and date of birth--might open an account in your name, change the mailing address, then run up charges on the account. You're completely in the dark that the identity fraud has happened.

1. How do I know if I am a victim of identity theft?

You may get a call from a company regarding a credit application they received that you did not fill out. You start getting bills from companies from whom you did not make a purchase. I suggest that you occasionally check your credit report to make sure all the information is correct.

2. How can I protect myself from identity theft?

There are several steps you can take to protect yourself. There are no guarantees, but fore-warned is fore armed.

 Don't keep unused bank accounts opened.

 Keep all of your personal information in a secure place.

 When you make a purchase with a credit card, ask for the carbon if they use them.

 Never give your personal information out over the phone.

 Review your credit card statements and other bills for any discrepancies or unusual activity, and report any problems immediately.

3. How do identity thieves work?

• They open a new credit card account, using your name, date of birth, and Social Security number. They use the credit card but don't pay the bills, and the delinquent account goes against your credit report.

• They call your credit card issuer, pretend to be you, and change the mailing address on your account. Then they max out your account, and the bill goes to the new address so you do not find out about the problem.

• They establish cellular phone service in your name.

• They open a bank account in your name and write bad checks on that account.

"In protecting your information, pick a password that will be easy for you to remember, but not one that someone could easily guess. "

4. I don't think I could be a victim of identity theft; I don't have a very high income. Could I be a target?

Anyone can be a victim--rich, poor, white collar, blue collar. As long as they can get ahold of your information, you can be a victim.

5. What should I do if I am a victim of identity theft?

There is a procedure to follow if you have been the victim of identity theft or suspect you have been. Depending on how your identity has been misrepresented, you many end up having to deal with many different organizations.

Call the three major credit bureaus. (They are listed in the Credit and Debt Chapter.) Tell them to place a fraud alert in your file that includes a statement that creditors should get your permission before opening any new accounts in your name. Each credit bureau has a fraud center on its web site that will direct you through its own procedure for filing and following up on a complaint.

Fill out an affidavit. All three credit bureaus offer a downloadable ID Theft Affidavit, which you should fill out and send according to the instructions.

Contact your creditors. Ask to speak to someone in the security or fraud department. Do a follow up letter so you have a hard copy. Also, call the companies you have credit with who have not been affected, and alert them to be on the lookout for anything suspect. If the thief can access one of your accounts, there is a chance he or she could gain access to others.

"You can never be too careful with your personal information."

File a report with your local police force. Even if they are not able to find the thief, you can use the police report as further evidence for your creditors or the credit bureaus that a crime was committed.

File a complaint with the Federal Trade Commission's Identity Theft Hotline. They will send you the forms required to lodge a formal complaint.

Call the Social Security Administration if someone has used your Social Security number to get a job or apply for credit. This will ensure that your wages are reported correctly.

6. Can getting a new Social Security number fix your credit report?

No, a new number will not fix your credit report, but a new number is given to victims who have made every possible effort to resolve the problem. You will not be granted a new number if you are in the following categories:

- You are trying to avoid the law.

- You want to cover up poor credit or a criminal record when you are at fault.

- You don't have proof that your number was abused, even if it was stolen or lost.

7. Is there a credit report monitoring program with which I can register?

There are several companies that work with the major credit bureaus to monitor credit reports for fraudulent activity. Privista is one of the companies and offers the following three services for a fee of $49.95 a year:

"ID Guard" is a product that is updated weekly to monitor your credit records for signs of identity theft. It will alert you by e-mail if there are any changes or new postings in your file that may be an indication of fraud. You can determine how strict the ID Guard alarms should be.

"Credit Insight" combines ID Guard with online access to your credit reports.

"Opt-Out Manager" is an automated tool that helps users reduce mass marketing and direct mailings.

8. I am looking for a new job. What questions should I ask to be sure my personal information will be protected by potential employers?

A new employer will need to have access to your personal information, so it is important to ask the right questions about their policies regarding this information.

"Don't assume that you will never become a victim of identity theft-- everyone is at risk."

Do they really need it?

Do they have security measurers to protect it?

Do they conduct background checks on those individuals who will have access to your personal information?

You will likely fill out an employment application requesting your Social Security number. Tell them you will provide it upon request, this way if you aren't hired, your number will not be hanging around the office.

9. Am I legally obligated to give out my Social Security number?

Many companies and associations will ask you to provide your Social Security number, but you are only obligated to give it to the Bureau of Motor Vehicles, tax departments and welfare departments. Since investment companies and banks are regulated, they too have a legitimate need for your Social Security number. Just remember, you can say no to schools, phone companies, health clubs, insurance companies and any other company that you feel does not need the number.

10. If I am a victim of identity theft, what is my liability?

Typically, if you are a victim of identity theft, you will not be charged for any purchases made using your stolen information. With the theft of your ATM card, if you report it missing within two days, you are only liable for $50.00. After that you will be liable for up to $500.00.

11. I have avoided shopping online for fear of identity theft. Is this a valid concern?

Yes, it is a valid concern. If you use a secure browser when you are shopping online, however, it will guard the security of your transactions. When submitting your purchase information, look for the "lock" icon on the browser's status bar to be sure your information is secure during your transaction.

12. I have been thinking about banking online to save time and money. Is this safe?

Yes, banks have spent years developing programs that will allow their clients the convenience of banking online. You can be assured that they have done what is possible to protect your information from potential identity theft. Sit down with your personal banker and ask any question you may have regarding the safety of banking online.

> **Identity theft is a serious concern.**
> You could be a victim for several days or even months if you are not diligent. Be a prudent consumer. Safe guarding your personal information is your responsibility, and it will fall on you to clean up the mess after you have been a victim.
> **Unfair, but true.**

C H A P T E R   9

Estate Planning

 There are only two sure things in this lifetime– death and taxes.

You may also have heard, "You can't take it with you." We spend our lives making money and buying stuff, but we don't take the time to think about what to do with it if we die. The perfect end would be to use up all that we have before we die. That would make life easy, but unfortunately, it doesn't happen that way. You will likely have something to leave behind, but with a little planning you will make the right decisions.

1. What is my "estate?"

Your estate consists of all of your assets and liabilities at the time of your death. Assets consist of property, investments, savings and any other valuables you own when you die. Your liabilities consist of your debts and financial obligations when you die. If you're married, you should take into consideration assets and liabilities of both parties.

2. What is a will?

A will is a written declaration of how you would like the assets of your estate distributed. Your will directs the probate court as to how to divide your assets and to whom they should be distributed. Often, the signing of the will must be witnessed by at least two other individuals, both of which should be neutral third parties. Keep in mind signing requirements may differ from state to state.

3. What is estate planning?

Estate planning is more than just making a will; it's a process of organizing your financial and personal interests in accordance with prevailing laws, so that your wishes are met with a minimum of inconvenience and expense to your family. It is also about accumulating wealth, preserving and protecting that wealth, and passing it on to your heirs. Estate planning is a key element in your financial planning that you shouldn't live or die without.

4. What do I need to think about in order to establish my estate plan?

There are several straightforward objectives to consider:

- Consider the financial responsibilities you will leave behind if you die. You will want to minimize the problems and expenses of probate court, to avoid potential family conflicts where possible, and to pass on your estate in accordance with your wishes.

- Determine the assets that you will want to

"Estate planning is something you will want to get right; you will not be around to correct any mistakes you make."

Estate planning can be empowering. It allows you to take care of those you love even after you are gone–and that brings peace of mind.

---

leave your family and/or friends. You will want to provide your spouse with as much responsibility and flexibility in estate management as desired, consistent with potential tax savings.

• Do what you can to minimize taxes at the time of death as well as estate taxes after death.

• Avoid leaving your children too much too soon.

• Provide adequate liquidity to cover taxes and other expenses at death without the necessity of a forced sale of assets.

• Provide for estate management if you do not have a spouse or in the event of the incapacity of your spouse.

• Organize all important papers affecting your estate plan in a location known to all family members, and review them at least annually.

• Inform all family members about the overall estate plan.

5. What expectations should I have when I set up my estate plan?

You should expect to preserve the value of your financial assets and make them easily accessible to your heirs. Your estate plan should take into account estate taxes and expenses, and provide for distribution of your assets after you die.

6. What can a will do?

A will can:

1. Make sure your heirs have the financial support they need.

2. Distribute assets to relatives or non-relatives according to your wishes.

3. Provide for charitable distributions.

4. Determine the executor of your estate.

5. Reduce the costs of settling your estate.

"Greed is a horrible thing. Get your family together in the same place when distributing your valuables-- they will thank you."

7. What happens if I die without a will?

Without a will, the probate court will make decisions on how your estate is to be distributed, and it may not be according to your wishes.

8. What if I draw up my will then change my mind?

You can change your will accordingly, at any time; it becomes final only when you die. You can make changes in two ways:

1 For big changes, you can draw up a new will and revoke the old one. The later date will be adequate proof, but you should destroy all old wills so there's no confusion.

2 If the changes are simple, you can easily add a codicil (an amendment) to your current will, and it will update effective the day you sign it.

9. When is it advisable to change my will?

It is a good idea to change your will when:

- You move to another state.

- You get married, divorced or have children.

- Your assets increase or decrease substantially.

- You decide on a different beneficiary, or the needs of your family changes.

- There is a change in the federal or state estate tax laws.

10. What is a trust?

 Think of a trust as a barn in which you place all of your assets, and from which you can maybe remove them as well.

The "maybe" is because there are two kinds of trusts.

An irrevocable trust allows assets to be taken in and out of the trust. It is the trust document itself that cannot be changed and is irrevocable.

A revocable trust allows you to make changes in your choices. But upon your death, your revocable trust becomes irrevocable, since you will not be around to make changes.

A trust is a legal document, and if it is funded, it

is responsible for paying taxes on earnings from its investment.

The most common trust is a *living trust*; it is used while you're still alive. You put everything into that trust, and you name a trustee. You can name yourself or someone else or even a bank. If you name yourself, you will need to name a successor trustee to take over if you become incapacitated or when you die. The trust holds and manages your assets for your benefit or for the beneficiaries while you are alive. For trusts in this category, the grantor of the trust remains personally liable for all tax liability associated with the assets in the trust during his or her lifetime.

11. What is a power of attorney?

Estate planning is more than passing assets to the next generation. It will provide the mechanisms for you, while you are in good health and of sound mind, to appoint a person to act on your behalf legally, financially, and most importantly medically, should you become ill.

A durable power of attorney is a legal document in which you designate someone to act on your behalf legally and financially. This person becomes your attorney-in-fact. You can limit this power or make it all-encompassing.

12. I want to pick the right executor. What responsibilities do they have?

Your executor should be the individual or organization that you trust to settle your estate according to your wishes. The executor's duties are as follows:

- Inventory all of your assets and liabilities.

- Sign the petition for the probate process, identifying the heirs and the provisions of your will.

- Formally notify all heirs and beneficiaries that your will is in probate.

- Settle all of the estate's accounts by paying debts and taxes.

- Distribute the remaining assets to your beneficiaries and make a final accounting of the estate to the court.

Choose your executor wisely. The individual or organization will be the one to distribute your assets to your heirs and settle legal or financial affairs.

Every one is different–you have different needs, assets and situations that will need to be considered while you plan for what happens when you are no longer here.

There are many more issues to consider when estate planning. Consulting an attorney who deals with these issues everyday is vital in order for you to be able to make the right decision for your situation. Your estate plan should be reviewed every year to keep up with any changes in your life, the laws or in estate taxes.

MONEY MADE $IMPLE

Angie Hollerich CEP, CCA

Angie is a professional speaker, and a published author. Her titles include: *Grab the Brass Ring of Financial Security©* , a self-help guide to a secure financial future; *The Weight and Wealth Factors©*, parallels for weight management and a healthy life; and *The Weight and Wealth Factors Strategy Boxes©* , health and financial strategies for The Graduate, Newlyweds, New Parents, Suddenly Single, Retiree and General; *The Wellness Path©* , twelve American experts reveal proven health and wellness strategies; and *Tips from the Top*, targeted finance advice from America's top money minds and *Mission Possible.* Her company, Brass Ring Productions, Ltd., provides programs to company owners and association leaders who understand the importance of education for their employees and members in the area of financial success, communications and personal development skills to increase productivity retention and attitude.

Angie has taken her life experiences, "good and bad", and developed thought-provoking programs that allow the participants to recognize their ability to overcome any obstacle that gets in their way. From strategic communication skills, to financial security, to health issues, Angie will provide the tools for individuals to take charge of their lives.

Presenting at conferences, Angie's down-to-earth style immediately engages her audiences and totally energizes them with her fun, interactive presentations and programs. Having worked as a financial advisor for ten years Angie recognized early in her career that successful financial strategies are a result of the ability to have answers to the many questions individuals have about their money. She enables individuals to understand and implement the answers in a manner that is fun and effective, with great success and higher productivity.

Angie is the first person to recognize and document the parallels between weight management and wealth accumulation, documented in her book *The Weight and Wealth Factors*. She is licensed with Herrmann International (HBDI); a Certified Educational Planner, Certified Women's Business Enterprise

(WBE); a member of the Association for
Financial Counseling and Planning Education
(AFCEP); 2003-2004 President, Ohio Chapter ~
National Speakers Association; professional
member of the National Speakers Association
and a member of the National Association of
Women Business Owners.

Angie Hollerich, Owner
Brass Ring Productions, Ltd.
P. O. Box 307318
Gahanna, Ohio 43230-7318
614/337/2204 (office)
614/337/2283 (fax)
www.brassringpro.com
angieh@brassringpro.com

ANGIE HOLLERICH CEP, CCA, CLL
AREAS OF EXPERTISE

Financial Success: Financial concerns affect your employee's productivity in this time of economic turmoil. Financial education is a vital part of your employee benefits package.

Grab the Brass Ring of Financial Security°
Street Smart Investing (Wall Street, That Is!)°
Making Dollars out of $ense°
Your Earned It...Don't You Want To Keep It?°
Manageable Money Matters°
College Prep: Higher Earning for Higher Learning°
Risk: For Reward Sake°
A Women's Worth: Your Future Deserves Your Time°
Cents and Sensibility°
The Psychology Of Money°
Money Made Simple°

Financial and health: Every year health care costs increase which affects the bottom line of a company's profit and loss statement. Employees who recognize areas of their health and wealth that need to be addressed become happier and more productive.

The Health and Wealth Factors°
(Can separate and do Health or Wealth separately)
The Inside Skinny to Health and Wealth°

Motivation & Laughter: What motivates you may not be what motivates your employees. A motivated employee is not only happier, but is well rounded and better able to handle unexpected obstacles that pop up in their everyday lives.

Track Your Mood to Train Your Mind°
What if you were Brave?°
Dream, Team, Dare, Care°
Laughter is the Best Medicine°

Communication: Did you know that we process and deliver information differently? A better understanding of our unique communication style will benefit your employee's ability to connect in the office and with your clients and customers.

Brain Power°
(As related to: Strategic Communication Skills, Non Traditional Sales)
Leadership, Team Building and Marketing°
Listening and Caring Skills

Sales & Marketing: Sales strategies for industries who can't market and sell in the traditional way.

Non-Traditional Sales Strategies°
How to Succeed in the Financial Industry°
Selling to Women°

*Programs developed for your specific situation and concerns.

Brass Ring Productions Ltd. P. O. Box 307318,
Gahanna, Ohio 43230-7318
614-337-2204   fax: 614-337-2283
www.brassringpro.com angieh@brassringpro.com

Order other publications from Brass Ring Productions!

PLEASE PRINT CLEARLY!

Name _____

Address _____

City/State/Zip _____

Phone _____ E-Mail _____

I would like to receive your e-newsletter   ○ Yes   ○ No

Description	Price	Quantity	Total
The Health & Wealth Factors® Book	$14.95		
The Weight & Wealth Strategy Boxes®			
The Graduate®	$14.95		
Newlyweds®	$14.95		
New Parents®	$14.95		
Suddenly Single®	$14.95		
Retiree®	$14.95		
General®	$14.95		
The Weight & Wealth Factors Journal®	$5.50		
Grab the Brass Ring Workbook	$19.95		
of Financial Security® CD	$14.95		
Money Made Simple	$12.95		
The Wellness Path	$12.95		
Track Your Mood to Change Your Mind®	$ 2.50		
Mission Possible	$15.95		

Order by Fax: Fax this form to 614-337-2283.

Order by Phone: Call 614-337-2204, have your credit card ready, please.

Order by Mail: Mail this form to:
Brass Ring Productions
P.O. Box 307318
Gahanna, Ohio 43230-7318

Subtotal	
Sales Tax add 6.75%	
S & H add $4.50	
TOTAL	

Payment Method

Quantity Discounts Available

Check one: ○ MC   ○ Visa   ○ AMX   ○ Check

Credit Card # _____

Expiration Date _____

Signature _____